MUSK-OXEN

MUSK-OXEN

MICHAEL GEORGE

THE CHILD'S WORLD

DESIGN
Bill Foster of Albarella & Associates, Inc.

PHOTO CREDITS
Joe Van Os: front cover, back cover, 2, 9,
11, 13, 14, 16, 21, 22, 25
Leonard Rue III: 6
The Zoological Society of San Diego: 18
George Herben: 26, 29, 30

Distributed to schools and libraries
in the United States by
ENCYCLOPAEDIA BRITANNICA EDUCATIONAL CORP
310 South Michigan Ave.
Chicago, Illinois 60604

Library of Congress Cataloging-in-Publication Data
George, Michael, 1964-
Musk-oxen/Michael George.
p. cm. — (Child's World Wildlife Library)
Summary: Describes the characteristics and behavior
of the musk-oxen.
ISBN 0-89565-721-X
1. Musk ox — Juvenile literature.   [1. Musk ox.]   I. Title.
II. Series.   91-13375
QL737.U53G46 1991   CIP
599.73'58—dc20   AC

For all who thrive in the cold and snow.

Ten thousand years ago, during the last ice age, the world was much different from what it is today. Snow and ice covered much of earth's surface. Woolly mammoths, saber-toothed tigers, and other strange animals roamed the frozen land. As time passed, the earth's climate grew warmer, and many of these cold-weather creatures disappeared. One of the few that remains is the musk-oxen.

Despite their name, musk-oxen do not smell musky nor are they oxen. Their closest relatives are goats. However, musk-oxen look more like long-haired buffalo. Male musk-oxen grow only four feet tall but weigh nearly 900 pounds. Female musk-oxen are slightly smaller than the males.

Both male and female musk-oxen have sharp, curved horns. Their horns join together to form a plate above the eyes. This plate is as thick as a dictionary and as hard as steel!

Musk-oxen live in the Arctic, the northernmost land in the world. The climate in the Arctic is like that of the ice ages long past. Winter lasts for eight months of the year. Snow and ice cover the ground, and the temperature drops far below zero.

Musk-oxen are well equipped to survive in the Arctic. On the outside, they wear a thick coat of shaggy brown hair. Beneath their long outer hairs, musk-oxen have a thick, woolly undercoat. It covers every part of a musk-ox except its lips and nostrils. This undercoat is far warmer than the best winter jacket. It keeps musk-oxen toasty even during the coldest arctic nights.

Musk-oxen live in herds that contain between 20 and 30 animals. During blizzards or extremely cold weather, musk-oxen huddle together. They turn their backs to the wind to stay extra warm. Sometimes the musk-oxen lie down in the snow to rest. When they wake up, their furry bodies are covered with windswept snow.

When the weather is nicer, herds of musk-oxen roam across the Arctic in search of food. Musk-oxen are *herbivores*, or plant eaters. The herds usually stay on top of low-lying hills where the wind uncovers frozen plants. When a thin layer of snow or ice covers the ground, the musk-oxen dig into it with their hooves. Sometimes they bang their chins against the hardened snow to uncover frozen plants.

In the Arctic, winter comes to an end slowly. Even in April, the temperature rarely rises above zero. But by May, the frozen land begins to thaw. Snowdrifts slowly melt, and plants begin to sprout new leaves. As spring arrives, musk-oxen begin to shed their warm, underlying fur. This prevents them from overheating during the warmer months of summer.

As the temperature rises and food becomes more plentiful, female musk-oxen have babies. Baby musk-oxen, called *calves*, are born with warm, woolly fur. The fur protects them in case winter makes an unwelcome return. At first, the newborn calves drink milk from their mothers. Within a couple of weeks, they begin to nibble on tender grass, shrubs, and tree shoots.

Young musk-oxen usually stay with their mothers for two years. During this time, the mothers teach their young how to survive in the Arctic. They show them how to find food and avoid enemies.

Wolves are one of the musk-oxen's worst enemies. They like to eat young calves. When a pack of wolves approaches a herd, the musk-oxen do not run away like other animals. Instead, they form a circle with all the adults facing outward. The calves huddle together in the middle. One by one, the adult musk-oxen charge at the wolves. They lower their heads and try to gouge the wolves with their sharp horns. Only rarely does a pack of wolves break through the circle of adult musk-oxen and reach the calves.

Although the musk-oxen's defense works well against wolves, it does not work so well against humans. Grouped in their huddle, musk-oxen are easy targets for hunters armed with guns. During the 1800s, explorers, whalers, and fur traders destroyed entire herds of musk-oxen. They hunted musk-oxen for their meat and warm fur. Some people captured calves and sold them to zoos.

By the early 1930s, musk-oxen were nearly extinct. Governments finally made it illegal to kill the threatened animals. Since then, the musk-oxen population has gradually grown. Today, the earth is home to about 90,000 musk-oxen. They are no longer in danger of extinction.

In recent years, people have begun to raise musk-oxen on farms. Musk-oxen are ideal farm animals. Because they are so well adapted to the arctic climate, they do not need to be housed in barns, even during the coldest winters. In addition, they eat the same kind of food that other farm animals eat. Domesticated musk-oxen are curious and friendly. They like to be petted and scratched behind the ears. A musk-ox may even come running when a person calls its name!

Musk-oxen are raised for their underlying fur. This fur, called *qiviut*, is softer and warmer than the finest wool. In addition, qiviut does not shrink like other fabrics. In harvesting qiviut, farmers cannot shear musk-oxen like they do sheep. If all their hair is cut off, musk-oxen can catch pneumonia and die. Rather than shearing the musk-oxen, workers simply comb the qiviut off the animals each spring. After the qiviut is cleaned, it is woven into scarves, hats, or sweaters.

Not too long ago, humans threatened to wipe the musk-oxen from the face of the earth. But through caring and protection, we have saved the musk-oxen from extinction. Today, musk-oxen provide us with warm clothing and friendly companionship. They also give us a glimpse of the far distant past. Musk-oxen are one of the few survivors from a time long ago.